Skills for Resolving

MW00686378

Communicating in a
Healthy Way

by

Marna Owen

GLOBE FEARON

Pearson Learning Group

Project Editors: Helene Avraham, Laura Baselice, Lynn W. Kloss
Executive Editor: Joan Carrafiello
Production Director: Penny Gibson
Production Editor: Nicole Cypher
Marketing Manager: Marjorie Curson
Interior Electronic Design: Patricia Smythe
Illustrator: Donna Nettis
Photo and Art Coordinator: Jenifer Hixson
Electronic Page Production: Eric Dawson
Cover Design: Eric Dawson
Cover Photograph: © Steve and Mary Beran Skjold

Reviewers:

Dorie L. Knaub, B.A., M.S.
Special Education Specialist
Downey Unified School District
Downey, California

Odalis Veronica Martin, B.A., M.S.
Special Education Teacher
Dade County Public Schools
Miami, Florida

Photo Credits: p. 12: Westerman and Associates/Liaison International; **p. 18**: © Jeffrey High, IMAGE Productions; **p. 26**: © Richard Hutchings, Photo Researchers; **p. 40**: © Radi Nabulsi; **p. 52**: © Pamela Marks Blanchard

Copyright © 1996 by Pearson Education, Inc., publishing as Globe Fearon, an imprint of Pearson Learning Group, 299 Jefferson Road, Parsippany, NJ 07054. All rights reserved. No part of this book may be reproduced or transmitted in any form or by any means, electronic or mechanical, including photocopying, recording, or by any information storage and retrieval system, without permission in writing from the publisher. For information regarding permission(s), write to Rights and Permissions Department.

ISBN 0-8359-1266-3
Printed in the United States of America
    9 10 11 12   06 05

Globe
Fearon

Pearson Learning Group

1-800-321-3106
www.pearsonlearning.com

Contents

Chapter 1

What is Healthy Communication?

Chapter Objectives

- Define communication.
- List five reasons that people communicate.
- Explain what it means to communicate in a healthy way.
- Identify communication styles.

Words to Know

communicate: to share or exchange information or ideas

message: the idea or information that the sender wants to share with the listener

interpret (ihn-TEHR-priht): to explain or understand the meaning of a message

positive: constructive, optimistic, or hopeful

negative: harmful; not helpful

instinct: responses of people or animals which are not learned, but are inborn

A Success Story

Martin's grades were not very high. His report card usually caused a fight between him and his father.

This year, Martin had done well in one class. It was a class about communication. Martin decided to put what he learned to a test. He wanted to talk to his father about his report card without fighting. He wanted to get his father's help. After some thought, here is what he did.

"Dad, I have something I want to talk to you about," Martin said.

Martin's dad looked up in surprise. Martin did not usually discuss much of anything with him.

"It's my report card," continued Martin. "It's about the same as usual. It's not very good. I want you to know how I feel about it. I don't like receiving poor grades. It's just that I have a hard time studying. Even when I do study, I don't do well on tests. I'm stuck, Dad. I could use your help."

Martin's dad was not sure what to say. His son had never seemed so serious.

"Well," Martin's dad said, clearing his throat. "Let's talk about it some more. You know, this is the first time I ever heard you say that your grades mattered to you. I thought they only mattered to me."

➤ Think About It

Do you think Martin and his dad are communicating in a healthy way? Why or why not?

_____

_____

What It Means to Communicate

Planning can help you make sure your message is understood.

Many of us wish we could communicate the way Martin did. To **communicate** is to share or exchange information or ideas. For communication to happen, there must be a sender, a message, and a listener. Each plays an important part in how poorly—or how well—people communicate.

The sender has the important role of presenting a clear message. Martin was a sender. He thought about the purpose of the talk. He prepared what he wanted to say. His father listened to him because Martin was serious. Martin's planning helped make the communication easier.

The **message** is the idea or information that the sender wants to share. Messages are usually made up of written or spoken words. Sometimes we send messages without saying anything. A sign that shows children walking, for example, tells drivers to slow down. We also send messages by the way we look or act. Suppose Martin had handed his father his report card, then started to cry. What message would he have sent?

The listener is the person who receives the message. A listener's role is to **interpret**, or understand, the meaning of a message. We "listen" to messages in many ways. When we are reading newspapers or books, we are listening. When we hear someone talking or singing, we are listening. We even listen through touching. An arm around our shoulder sends the message that someone cares.

➤ Senders, Messages, and Listeners

In each of the examples below, identify the sender, message, and listener.

1. Sara asks Kyle to go to a movie with her.

Sender: _____

Message: _____

Listener: _____

2. Leon yawns during his sister's music recital. His sister sees him.

Sender: _____

Message: _____

Listener: _____

3. A friend writes you a letter about her sick cat.

Sender: _____

Message: _____

Listener: _____

4. You are reading this book.

Sender: _____

Message: _____

Listener: _____

Why We Communicate

Before Martin talked to his father, he identified a communication goal. He wanted to let his father know how he felt. He wanted to get help from him. He wanted to communicate without a fight.

Whenever you communicate, you have a goal. Often, you are not aware of that goal. You may talk to friends, laugh, or sing without thinking about what you're trying to do. Usually, you're communicating with one or more of these goals in mind:

- To let others know how you feel
- To get to know someone
- To teach
- To learn
- To solve problems
- To have fun

Can you add to this list?

Communication is an important part of every person's life. Think of how many times you communicate every day! Communication helps you in your friendships, families, school, and work. It helps you say who you are and what you mean. Without it, the world would be a quiet, lonely place.

➤ **Your Communication Goal**

Answer these questions about your communication goals on the lines provided.

1. Think about your last phone call. What was your communication goal?

_____

_____

2. Think about the last thing you read. What was your communication goal?

_____

_____

3. Think about the last thing you wrote. What was your communication goal?

_____

_____

4. Think about the last thing you listened to. What was your communication goal?

_____

_____

Healthy Communication

Martin and his father communicated in a healthy way. Communication is healthy when it helps to achieve goals in a **positive**, or constructive, way. Martin achieved his goal by being honest. He talked to his father with respect. His father returned that respect. These positive practices helped Martin to achieve his goal.

Suppose Martin had lied or called his father names? He would have been communicating in an unhealthy way. Such **negative**, or harmful, practices can cause fights, misunderstandings, and missed opportunities. They get in the way of achieving a goal.

➤ Looking for Healthy Ways to Communicate

Read each set of statements. Circle the example of healthy communication.

1. **a.** "You're in my way!"
   b. "Please excuse me."
   c. "I need to get by."

2. **a.** "What are you talking about?"
   b. "You're not making any sense."
   c. "Could you explain that again, please?"

3. **a.** "Just forget it."
   b. "Let's talk about this later when I'm not so upset."
   c. "I don't care. Do what you want."

4. **a.** "You've already made up your mind."
   b. "It's your choice. I want you to think about what might happen if you do it your way."
   c. "If you don't do what I say, you'll be sorry."

Communication Styles

This book explores how a person can develop a healthy communication style. Your style has to do with the way you communicate. It has to do with how you hold yourself, your tone of voice, the words you choose, and how well you listen. Communication styles are powerful. They can either create problems or solve problems. They can help listeners get the right message or put up walls between people.

Working through this book will help you develop a healthy communication style.

How can a communication style create problems? How can it solve them?

Your communication style should:
- Help you achieve your goals.
- Show respect for yourself and others.
- Keep the lines of communication open.

Learning and practicing new ways of communicating is not easy. But, it can be done. As a baby, you communicated by **instinct**. You used inborn responses to communicate your needs to those around you. When you were hungry, you cried. When you were happy, you smiled. Later, you learned to show how you felt by imitating others. Eventually, you learned to talk, to read, and to write.

Now that you know "how" to communicate, think about the way you communicate. Working through this book will make you aware of what you do, how you act, and what you say. It will help you practice ways of getting your messages across.

➤ Thinking About Your Communication Style

Think about times you communicated with others. Think about how you used your body, your voice, and your words. Think about how others reacted to you. Use these experiences to help you finish the following sentences.

1. When I am happy, I communicate it by _____

_____

This usually causes others to _____

2. When I am scared, I communicate it by _____

_____

This usually causes others to _____

3. When I am angry, I usually communicate it by _____

_____

This usually causes others to _____

_____

4. When I am sad, I usually communicate it by _____

_____

This usually causes others to _____

_____

Chapter Summary

- Communication is the sharing or exchanging of information and ideas. All forms of communication involve a sender, a message, and a listener. Communication happens when you read, write, speak, listen, touch, feel, or look a certain way.
- You communicate to achieve goals. The most common communication goals are to let others know how you feel, to get to know others, to teach, to entertain, to learn, or to solve problems.
- Healthy communication happens when you try to achieve your goals in positive ways. Being honest, talking about your feelings, and asking for help are three examples of healthy communication.
- Your communication style can help communication or hurt it. Your style can cause others to fight back, withdraw, or listen openly. Communication style has to do with how you use your body, your tone of voice, the words you use, and how carefully you listen.

Chapter Review

Words to Know

Complete each sentence with one of the following words:

communicate   instinct   interpret

positive   negative   message

1. To exchange information is to _____.

2. _____ causes a baby to cry when hungry.

3. When something is helpful, it is _____.

4. When you _____ what someone says, you understand the meaning of the message.

5. When something is harmful, it is _____.

6. When someone sends you a _____, he or she is sharing information with you.

About Communication

Answer each question on the lines provided.

1. What is healthy communication? _____

_____

2. Name three things that make up your communication style. _____

_____

Chapter 2

Body Language

Chapter Objectives

- Explain how you use your body while communicating.
- Identify messages that you send with your body.
- Use body language that matches your words.

Words to Know

body language: how people use their bodies to
   communicate

impression (ihm-PREHSH-uhn): an effect produced
   on the mind or the feelings

Say It Without Words

Laura was new at the high school. She felt
shy and unsure of herself. Her teacher paired
her with a classmate named Bev. They had to
work on a class project together.

Laura stared at the floor to hide her
uneasiness. She waited for Bev to say
something.

Bev looked at Laura. She thought Laura
seemed stuck up. This made her angry. She
didn't want to work with someone who seemed
to dislike her.

Bev crossed her arms and legs. She
tightened her mouth. "Well, how should we do
this?" she asked in a flat voice. Laura looked up
and saw Bev's crossed arms and angry face.
This made her even more nervous.

"I don't know," Laura replied. She looked
down again.

"Well," said Bev, pulling her arms closer.
"I'm not going to do all the work."

The two girls sat side by side without saying
a word. At the end of the period, the teacher
came by. She saw that nothing had been
accomplished.

"You two will have to work on this again
tomorrow," the teacher said. "Every pair of
students must complete the assignment."

Bev and Laura both groaned. Another day
of this! What would they do?

If you were friends with Bev and Laura, what advice would you give them? Why?

_____

_____

Body Language

Bev and Laura could both learn how their **body language** affects communication. Body language is how we use our bodies to send messages without talking. When Laura looked at the floor, she sent the message, "I'm shy." Bev interpreted this as "She doesn't like me." When Bev crossed her arms, Laura interpreted the action as "She doesn't like me." Body language completely stopped their communication.

How do you know when someone isn't telling the truth?

How you stand, sit, use your arms, or shape your face are examples of body language. Body language is an important part of your communication style. Experts say that people watch and "listen" to body language even more than they do words or tone of voice!

To be a better communicator, you should be aware of how your body language may be seen by others. Then you can use body language to help you accomplish your goals—not get in the way!

You cannot always know how a listener will interpret your body language. But you can make some good guesses. The following chart lists possible messages sent by different body actions.

Remembering these messages may help you keep lines of communication open!

When You:	Listeners Might Think You Are Saying:
Cross your arms	Don't talk to me! I don't trust you. You have to convince me!
Yawn	I'm tired. I'm bored. I'm not interested.
Point at your listener	I'm right. You'd better listen to me!
Stare	Don't get smart with me. Be careful what you say! I can't believe this!

➤ Put It to Work

Show a classmate each type of body language listed in the chart below. Ask your partner to describe the message received. Record the message in the chart. You may choose to complete the activity on your own by viewing your actions in a mirror.

When You: **Listener Received the Message:**

Look at the floor   _____

                              _____

                              _____

Frown   _____

                              _____

                              _____

Quickly blink your eyes   _____

                              _____

                              _____

Put your hands on your hips   _____

                              _____

                              _____

Shake a fist   _____

                              _____

                              _____

Positive Body Language

So far, you've explored body language that may "turn off" the listener. Sometimes, body language can improve communication or make it better. The chart below lists some examples of positive body language.

When You:	Listener Might Get the Message:
Sit up straight	I'm confident. I'm listening.
Smile	It's safe to talk to me. I'm friendly.
Hold your hands open as you speak	I am sincere. I care about what I'm saying.
Nod your head as you talk	I'm interested in what you have to say. I agree with you.

➤ Communication Builder

Complete this activity with a classmate. Begin by reading the situations described on the next page. Then:

a. Identify the sender and listener in each situation. List two ways the sender could use body language to send a positive message.

b. Act out the first situation with your partner. One person should act as the sender while the other acts as the listener. Remember to use positive body language.

c. After you act out the situation, have the listener describe the message received from the sender's body language.

d. Switch roles and act out the next situation.

1. You are meeting a possible employer for the first time. How will you walk into her office?

What body language will the sender use?

_____

_____

What message did the listener receive?

_____

_____

2. You have to give a speech to the class. How will you walk to the front of the room? How will you stand as you deliver the speech?

What body language will the sender use?

_____

_____

What message did the listener receive?

_____

_____

3. A new student is carrying a tape by a performer you like. You think this person might become a friend. How would you approach this person?

What body language will the sender use?

_____

_____

What message did the listener receive?

_____

_____

Matching Words with Body Language

Remember the story about Bev and Laura? These classmates were having difficulty working together on a project. Their body language was interrupting their communication.

On the second day of the project, Bev sat down with Laura. She sighed and then looked away. Without looking at her partner, Bev said, "OK, let's get started. I really want to work with you today."

Laura did not believe Bev. While her words sent one message, Bev's body language sent the opposite message. Her words indicated she wanted to work with Laura, but her actions indicated she was bored and uninterested in Laura. Bev communicated mixed messages to her listener.

It is important for your body language to match your words. If it does not, the listener will not believe, trust, or be interested in what you have to say. This is what happened between Bev and Laura. If Bev had looked at Laura, smiled, and then spoke, Laura probably would have felt she meant what she said.

Matching your words with your body language is an important communication skill. It takes practice. But it is worth the effort! This skill will help you make a good **impression**, or have a good effect on the mind or feelings of your listeners. It will help you keep your listeners focused on what you are saying, even if they don't like what you have to say. It will help others to work with you. With a little body language, you can communicate a lot!

What body language would be most effective during a job interview?

➤ Communication Builder

Read each of the following statements. Identify one way you would use your body to make the message believable.

1. "I really enjoyed that movie."

_____

_____

2. "I'm pretty sure I could do this job."

_____

_____

3. "I agree with what you are saying."

_____

_____

4. "I think I'm ready for that responsibility."

_____

_____

➤ Communication in Action

Now say the first statement to a classmate. Use the body language listed for the statement. Ask your partner if your body language matched your words. Record their responses below. Switch roles and repeat the process for the other statements.

1. _____

2. _____

3. _____

4. _____

Chapter Summary

- The messages you send with your body are called body language. When you communicate with others, your listeners learn a great deal from the way you use your body. For this reason, you should be aware of your body language. You can use it to keep communication open and positive.
- You send many kinds of messages with your body. Listeners may interpret these messages in different ways. For example, crossing your arms may be seen as a sign that you are not ready to talk or listen. Looking at the floor may be seen as a sign of discomfort. Sitting straight and smiling may be seen as signs that you are listening.
- You should use body language that matches your words. Doing so will help your listener believe and trust you. Your listener will take what you say more seriously.

Chapter Review

Words to Know

Use your own words to define each term in the space provided.

1. body language _____

2. impression _____

About Body Language

Listed below are six examples of body language. Write the actions that could keep communication open in the first column. Write the actions that could close communication in the second column.

smiling   walking tall   looking down

sitting straight   crossing arms   frowning

OPEN   **CLOSE**

_____   _____

_____   _____

_____   _____

Getting Personal

List three ways you can use your body language to send positive messages.

_____

_____

_____

Chapter 3

Choosing Your Words with Care

Chapter Objectives

- Explain how words and tone of voice affect communication.
- Use a tone of voice that keeps communication open and positive.
- Use words and phrases that keep communication open and positive.

Words to Know

conversation: a spoken exchange of information or ideas

express: to state one's thoughts or feelings

react: to respond to what someone says or does

emotion (ih-MOH-shuhn): a strong feeling, such as love, hate, sadness, or anger

Making a Point

Mark and Sylvia had made plans to go out one Sunday. But Mark did not show up. He had been watching football with his friends, and he forgot about their date.

Sylvia was angry and hurt. She waited to speak with Mark until she could control her feelings. She thought about what she wanted to say. Their **conversation**, or their spoken exchange of ideas, went as follows:

"Mark," Sylvia said in an even voice. "I'm really disappointed that you didn't show up on Sunday."

"Well, I'm sorry," said Mark. "I forgot."

"I know," said Sylvia. "I still want you to know how I felt. I felt like I wasn't important to you."

Mark grunted.

Sylvia felt herself getting angry. She took a deep breath.

"If we make a date, I want you to keep it," said Sylvia. "If you can't keep it, I want you to call me and let me know."

"And if I don't?" Mark replied.

"That's not the point," responded Sylvia. "I'm letting you know what I want. Can you do that?"

Mark sighed. "I can do that. It was stupid and rude of me to have missed our date. I'm sorry. I won't let it happen again."

➤ **What Do You Think?**

Do you think Sylvia communicated in a healthy way? Why or why not?

_____

_____

How Important Are Words?

Sylvia did a good job communicating her feelings to Mark. She chose her words carefully. She said them carefully. Even though Mark was not happy about the conversation, Sylvia kept his attention. In doing so, she was able to meet her communication goal. She was successful in letting Mark know just how she felt about the missed date.

How can your tone of voice help your listener understand your message?

You have already learned that listeners learn a great deal about your message from your body language. What makes up the rest of the message? It comes from your tone of voice and the words you choose. When you use these things well, you can **express** yourself, or state your thoughts, better. Using a certain tone of voice and carefully selecting your words will help keep your listener focused on your message. These things will help your listener better understand your ideas and feelings. They will also help you reach your communication goal.

1. Think about a time when you stopped listening to someone. What did the speaker do or say to make you **react**, or respond, in that way?

_____

_____

2. Think about a time when you listened carefully to a speaker. What did the person do or say to keep you focused and make you want to listen?

_____

_____

_____

Your Tone of Voice

When Sylvia talked to Mark, she used an even, serious tone of voice. Why? She wanted Mark to know she meant what she said. She knew that if she sounded angry, Mark would become angry in return. These negative feelings would interrupt their communication. Sylvia's tone of voice kept Mark focused on what she said. It helped Mark listen. It helped them communicate.

Your tone of voice is almost as important as your body language. It sends a powerful message to the listener. Like body language, people tend to trust and listen to the tone of voice more than they do the words. Imagine that someone is saying "I love you" in a voice that is tense or bored. It would be hard for anyone to believe those words.

Imagine that someone said, "I'm really, really mad at you" in a cheerful tone of voice. What message would you receive? Why?

_____

_____

_____

A Clear Picture

When you are communicating, try to match your message with your tone of voice. If you talk in a light, happy tone, your message should also be light. If you have something important to say, use a serious tone. Be careful not to use too much **emotion**, or strong feeling, when speaking. Strong emotions can cause a listener to withdraw or become emotional. That is why Sylvia waited to speak with Mark until she could control her anger. If she had spoken with him earlier, she probably wouldn't have reached her communication goal. The only thing she would have communicated would have been her anger.

Does that mean you should never cry? Never get angry? Never lose control? That would be a difficult task for anyone. Every once in a while, people do let their angry feelings out. But as a rule, try to be aware of your feelings. Try to communicate them in a way that helps you achieve your goals.

➤ Communication in Action

Imagine that you promised your friend that you would attend a meeting. You lost track of the time and missed the meeting. Now your friend is angry with you.

a. Act out this situation with your partner taking the role of the angry friend. Show strong emotions when acting out the scene.

b. Switch roles and act out the situation again. This time, use a tone of voice that does not show strong emotions.

c. Think about how you felt each time you acted out the situation. Did your partner's tone of voice have an affect on you? Explain.

_____

_____

_____

Words That Get in the Way

Certain words and phrases can close the door to communication. They can create problems rather than solve them. They can cause listeners to feel attacked or belittled. Here are some examples of negative words:

How do you feel when someone says these things to you? Do you want to listen to the person?

- Blaming: "It's all your fault. This never would have happened if you were doing your job!"
- Name-calling: "You idiot! I can't believe how stupid you are!"
- Unhelpful criticism: "You're really bad at this, aren't you? I don't know how you ever got on the team."
- The words *always* and *never*: "We *always* have to do it your way! We *never* do it my way!"

Think about how you feel and react when you hear these words. Then become aware of when you use them. Being aware of your actions is the first step to change!

➤ **Communication Builder**

Circle the words or phrases that hurt communication in this conversation.

Sylvia was angry at Mark for breaking their date. She stormed over to his house and banged on the door.

"Open the door, you jerk!" she screamed.

Mark opened the door. "Pipe down. You'll wake up my brother."

"Who cares? You are thoughtless, so why shouldn't I be? You ruined my weekend. It's all your fault."

"I'm sorry," said Mark. "But that's the way it is."

"Oh, right," replied Sylvia. "It's always your way. It's never my way."

"What are you talking about? We always do things your way."

"You are so mean," yelled Sylvia. "You care more about your friends than you do about me!"

Mark was disgusted. "What do you want me to do? Give up my whole life? I don't want to talk about this anymore."

"See?" said Sylvia. "I knew you didn't care!"

➤ Think About It

What advice would you give Sylvia about her communication style?

_____

_____

Words that Work

Luckily, there are words that help communication. Here are some tips for keeping communication open and helping others to listen.

- Use words that focus on the problem and a possible solution.

  "Here's what I would like to see happen."

  "I'd like to get this problem fixed."

  "I know I made a mistake. I'm ready to apologize and work things out."

- Use the word, *I* instead of *you* as much as possible. In this way, the listener does not feel blamed for the problem.

  "I feel really angry about what happened."

  "I'm having a hard time understanding what you are saying."

- Use *often* or *sometimes* instead of *never* or *always*. This will prevent arguments about numbers.

  "I *often* get the feeling that you don't like me."

  "*Sometimes*, I feel like we just don't get along."

- Try using *and* instead of *but*. The word *but* can make listeners feel that you think what they said or did is unimportant.

  "I understand how you feel, *and* I want you to understand how I feel, too."

  "That's one way to look at it. *And* here's another way."

Which would you prefer to hear: "You're wrong" or "I'd like to see that done in a different way"? Why?

➤ Communication Builder

Read the following conversation between Bill and one of his workers named Joe. Underline the words or phrases that keep this communication positive.

BILL: I noticed that you were late again today. I'd like you to be on time more often.

JOE: You're always watching me! Do you have something against me?

BILL: I'm the boss. I expect all of my workers to be on time. Now let's talk about what's making you late.

JOE: You never notice when I'm on time.

BILL: Sometimes you are on time. I'd like you to come to work on time more often.

JOE: The problem is that my bus is hardly ever on time. The bus driver is a real flake!

BILL: What could you do to be on time regularly?

JOE: Well, I guess I could take an earlier bus.

BILL: Great! I think that sounds like a good idea. I'll make it a point to notice when you're on time!

➤ Communication in Action

Act out the conversation above with a partner. Use a tone of voice and body language that matches the words spoken. Upon completing the activity, record the message received by Bill and Joe.

BILL: _____

_____

JOE: _____

_____

Chapter Summary

- Your tone of voice and the words you choose are an important part of your communication style. Like body language, they can make your communication more positive and healthy. When your words are angry and hurtful, they can cause your listeners to stop communicating.

- Listeners will believe a tone of voice before they believe words. Good communicators use a tone of voice that matches their words. They keep their emotions under control, especially when they try to solve problems.

- When you blame others, name-call, give unhelpful criticism, and use words such as *never* and *always*, you hurt communication. Such words cause a listener to fight back or withdraw. On the other hand, choosing words that focus on goals, using *I* instead of *you*, using the word *and* instead of *but*, can improve communication. They help a listener remain open to what is being said.

Chapter Review

Words to Know

Match each word on the left with its meaning on the right. Write the correct letter in the space provided.

_____ **1.** conversation   **a.** a strong feeling

_____ **2.** emotion   **b.** to state one's feelings

_____ **3.** react   **c.** spoken exchange of ideas

_____ **4.** express   **d.** to respond to what someone says or does

About Words

Rewrite each statement so that it keeps communication open and positive.

1. "You fool! That's not how you throw a ball!"

_____

_____

2. "You never listen to me."

_____

_____

3. "Your idea is OK but mine is better."

_____

_____

Chapter 4

Listening

Chapter Objectives

- Explain why listening skills are important to healthy communication.
- Describe a "listening attitude."
- Practice three listening skills.

Words to Know

attitude: a person's way of acting, feeling, or thinking

encouragement (ihn-KEHR-ihj-muhnt): hope, confidence, or support

sincere (sihn-SEER): truthful or honest

What's Wrong With This Picture?

Miles wanted to stay out late one Saturday night. As he approached his mother, he said to himself, "I don't know why I'm doing this. She's never going to listen to me."

Miles hesitated, then he blurted out, "It's really important that I be able to stay out until midnight on Saturday. I'd like to get your permission."

"Midnight!" gasped his mother. "Absolutely not."

"You don't understand," Miles replied. "They're having a special Halloween dance at school. There's going to be a costume contest. If you're not there at midnight, you can't win."

"If you ask me," said his mother, "the school is asking for trouble."

Miles didn't give up. "Mom, I have a great costume. I'm going as a TV newscaster. Look, I built this cardboard TV to wear around my head. Don't I look great?"

His mother stared as he put on the costume.

"This really is important to me," Miles repeated.

"The answer is no and don't ask me again," said his mother.

Miles walked away angry. "I knew she wouldn't let me go," he fumed.

The Importance of Listening

Something was missing from Miles's conversation with his mother. Neither of them was listening! For communication to happen, there must be a sender, a message, and a listener. In a conversation, each person will take turns being the sender and the listener. You send a message. Your partner listens, then sends a message back.

Miles and his mother were hearing each other's words. But they weren't really listening to one another. Miles's mother did not understand how important the dance was to her son. Miles did not understand his mother's concern about the "school asking for trouble." If they had talked about these things, the outcome might have been different.

Good listening skills can help you better understand what others are telling you. You can then show them that you understand. This will strengthen your communication skills.

Good listening skills can help you communicate effectively.

➤ Rate Your Listening Skills

Take a moment to rate your listening skills on a scale of 1 to 5. For each item, circle the number that best describes you. Circle *1* if the statement *never* applies to you. Circle *5* if the statement *always* applies to you.

1. I pay attention when others talk.

1	2	3	4	5
Never		Regularly		Always

2. I listen to people who disagree with me.

1	2	3	4	5
Never		Regularly		Always

3. I listen as much as I talk.

1	2	3	4	5
Never		Regularly		Always

➤ **Write a Listening Goal**

How did you rate your listening skills? If you rated yourself *4* or above on any item, you already have good listening skills. If you rated yourself *3* or lower on any item, you probably should work on improving your skills. Write a listening goal for yourself on the lines below.

_____

_____

Have a Listening Attitude

Before Miles talked to his mother, he said to himself, "I don't know why I'm doing this. She's never going to listen to me."

Now suppose Miles had thought this instead: "I want to listen to my mother's concerns. If I understand her better, maybe we can work something out." He would have approached his mother with a different **attitude**, or way of feeling and acting. He would have been prepared to listen to her. This "listening attitude" would have kept communication open and positive.

How does one get a positive "listening attitude"? Here are some guidelines:

- Respect what others have to say.
- Be willing to change your communication goal based on what you learn.
- Don't assume that a person will behave in a certain way or know certain things. If you do, you may miss important information. Keep an open mind.
- Don't let your emotions keep you from hearing what a person says. If you cannot keep your emotions in check, end the conversation. Calm yourself down and then try again.

How can you put these guidelines into practice? Try this. Before talking to someone say to yourself, "I'm going to listen. I will respect what this person has to say. Together, we can find a way to make things work out."

Of course, you'll still have to work at listening. But by *choosing* to listen beforehand, your task will be easier.

Next time you're talking with someone, try one of these guidelines to help you communicate your message.

➤ Prepare Your Attitude

The following statements are things you might say to yourself before a conversation. Check the statements that would help you have a positive "listening attitude."

1. _____ "This is going to be a disaster."

2. _____ "I'm looking forward to hearing what he has to say."

3. _____ "If she calls me a name, I'm going to hit the roof."

4. _____ "I'm sure there is a way we can work this out."

5. ____ "I'm going to focus on working out this problem."

6. ____ "If I feel myself getting angry, I'll say so. Then I'll suggest talking later when I'm more in control of my feelings."

7. ____ "I think I'll be able to get to the bottom of this if I just listen to what she says."

8. ____ "No matter what I say, he won't listen to me."

9. ____ "Talking to him is probably a waste of time. He's such an airhead!"

10. ____ "Even though it won't do much good, I'll try to talk to her."

Let Them Know You Are Listening

When you are communicating, it is important to let the other person know you are listening. This helps to keep a discussion going. How do you show that you are listening? Think about what you already know. Use positive body language. Nod your head as the person talks. Make eye contact without staring. Sit forward or stand tall.

Your tone of voice can also show that you are listening. Depending on what you are talking about, try to sound serious or friendly.

You can also use phrases of **encouragement**, or support. Phrases such as "That's interesting," "Tell me more", and "I really want to hear what you have to say" show the person you are listening to their message.

It is important to be **sincere**, or honest, when using such phrases. If you don't really mean the words, don't say them. Honesty is necessary to good communication. Without it, it's hard to keep communication lines open.

➤ Communication in Action

Complete this activity with a partner. Follow these steps:

1. Ask your partner to tell you about an important day in his or her life.

2. As your partner talks, use:
   - "listening" body language
   - a serious and friendly tone of voice
   - words that encourage your friend to share his or her thoughts and feelings

3. When your partner is finished telling the story, ask:
   - Did you feel that I was listening to you?
   - How did I show a "listening attitude"?
   - What could I do to become a better listener?

4. Summarize the observations of both the speaker and listener on the lines below.

Speaker: _____

_____

_____

_____

_____

Listener: _____

_____

_____

_____

_____

Show You Understand

A key listening skill is understanding the speaker's ideas and feelings. Another key skill is *showing* the speaker that you understand! Let's see how the conversation between Miles and his mother might have gone if he had shown such understanding.

MILES: I really want to go to the Halloween dance. At midnight, they'll award prizes for the best costumes. You must be there to win. I think I have a good chance at winning. Could I have permission to stay out until midnight this Saturday?

MOM: No. That's too late. The school is asking for trouble.

MILES: What do you mean?

MOM: The last time they had a late night dance, there was trouble in the parking lot. Some students were hurt.

MILES: So, you think I'll get hurt if I stay late?

MOM: That's right. Besides, a rule is a rule.

MILES: I agree, Mom. A rule is a rule. I wouldn't make staying out late a habit. I understand you are worried about me. What would help you know that I am safe?

MOM: Well, what teachers are going to be there? Maybe if I called one . . .

When you repeat a person's words, it is called *mirroring*.

In this example, Miles shows he understands his mother's worries. By doing so, he is more likely to work out a solution with his mother.

How do you gain a clear understanding of what a speaker is saying? How do you show you understand?

One way is to repeat the words the person says. Miles did this when he said, "That's right, Mom. A rule is a rule." He showed his mother he agreed with her.

Another way is to repeat what the person says in your own words. This will show the speaker that you are listening carefully. Miles did this when he said, "So, you think I'll get hurt if I stay out late?" Miles was trying to find out what was really bothering his mother. By doing this, he helped make their communication clearer. He got to the root of the problem—his mother's concern for his safety.

➤ What Would You Say?

How would you respond to each of the following statements? Remember,
your response should help you understand the person's ideas and feelings.

1. JACK: I don't want you near that guy. He likes you too much.

   JILL: _____

   _____

2. TEACHER: I've had it. Every time I try to help you, you start acting like
   this.

   STUDENT: _____

   _____

3. DAD: I don't want you hanging out with that kid. He's bad news.

SON: _____

_____

4. EMPLOYER: How many times do I have to tell you to take out the garbage
at the end of your shift?

WORKER: _____

_____

Chapter Summary

- Listening skills help you better understand what others are telling you. They open the door to healthy communication.
- People with "listening attitudes" respect what others have to say. They have an open mind and are flexible about their goals. They do not assume what others know or how others will behave. They are prepared to learn. They do not let their emotions get in the way of communication.
- Listening skills include using open body language and a tone of voice that matches your message. Using words of encouragement, such as "Please tell me more," show the speaker that you are listening. When listening, you should attempt to understand the speaker's ideas and feelings. This can be done by repeating the speaker's words in your own words.

Chapter Review

Words to Know

Match each word on the left with its meaning on the right. Write the correct letter in the space provided.

_____ **1.** attitude   **a.** hope, confidence, or support

_____ **2.** encouragement   **b.** truthful

_____ **3.** sincere   **c.** a way of acting, feeling, or thinking

About Listening

Write four things you can do to be a better listener.

1. _____

2. _____

3. _____

4. _____

Getting Personal

Describe a situation in your life that might improve if you changed your "listening attitude."

_____

_____

_____

_____

_____

Chapter 5

Putting It All Together

Chapter Objectives

- Review key communication skills.
- Use positive communication skills in sample situations.
- Apply communication skills to real-life situations.

Words to Know

conscious (KAHN-shuhs): knowing what one is
doing and why

When Change is Hard

Nila had always been a kind person. Her
best friend, Lisa, knew this. Little by little, Lisa
began to abuse Nila's kindness. She asked to
borrow Nila's clothes, then she didn't return
them. She asked Nila to drive her places, but
she never paid for gas. She asked to copy Nila's
homework, and Nila let her.

Nila knew that she was being treated
poorly. But she found it difficult to say no. After
all, Lisa was her best friend.

One day, Lisa came to Nila with a plan. She
wanted to tell her parents that she was
spending Saturday night with Nila. Actually,
Lisa was going to attend a big party. She
wanted to stay out all night. She needed Nila to
go along with the lie.

Nila was uncomfortable with the plan. She
knew it was wrong. Yet, she couldn't say no to
Lisa.

Nila realized she had to change. She
couldn't let Lisa keep using her. Nila had to
figure out how to stand up for herself.

➤ Think About It

What advice would you give Nila?

_____

_____

A Quick Review

Nila's communication style needs some work. She is unable to say what she believes. She is unable to stand up for herself against Lisa.

This book has described a number of ways to communicate in a healthy way. Many of these methods could be helpful to Nila. This chapter reviews these communication skills. Why? Remember, communication styles are hard to change. You may have been communicating for years in ways that aren't always helpful. The only way to change is to practice! This quick review will provide you with an opportunity for guided practice. Then you will be on your own!

How could Nila improve her communication skills?

Review Communication Goals

Having goals is probably the most important part of healthy communication. Knowing what you want is the first step towards achieving it.

You also must believe in your goals. Changing your communication style is hard. Sometimes you will be successful. Sometimes you won't. To keep moving towards change, you must be committed to what you want to do.

In Nila's case, she might try putting her goal in writing. She could pin it on a wall where she would see it everyday. She could say it to herself every morning and night. By keeping her goal foremost in her mind, she would be more likely to work toward change. This will help her deal with Lisa.

➤ Communication Builder

1. Identify Nila's communication goal.

_____

_____

_____

2. List three things that Nila could do to be more committed to this goal.

_____

_____

_____

3. Write a communication goal for yourself.

_____

_____

_____

4. List three things that you will do to help yourself reach this goal.

_____

_____

_____

Review Body Language

When you communicate, people get over half of your message through body language. Body language can show your listeners that you are confident, know what you're talking about, and are ready to listen. It can also cause your listeners to "turn off." As with goals, you must be aware of your body language. You must make a **conscious**, or knowing, effort to change.

➤ **Practice Body Language**

1. What body language could Nila use when she talks to Lisa? Identify three things you would advise her to do.

_____

_____

_____

Review Tone of Voice and Words

Your tone of voice and your choice of words are as important as body language. A serious message deserves a serious tone of voice. A happy message deserves a happy tone of voice. An important rule is don't let your tone of voice show too much emotion.

Remember to keep focused on your goal when you choose words. Try repeating your goal statement during a conversation to focus both you and your listener. Use *I* instead of *you* as much as possible. Use *and* instead of *but*. Stay away from the words *always* and *never*. Following these guidelines helps keep communication open.

How would you change this sentence to achieve your communication goal: "You're always late!"?

➤ Communication Builder

1. What tone of voice should Nila use when she speaks with Lisa? Why?

_____

_____

2. Circle the statement you think Nila should use when she discusses her feelings with Lisa.

    a. "You are always using me."

    b. "I'm uncomfortable with your plan for Saturday night. I don't want to be involved."

    c. "If you really are my friend, you wouldn't ask me to do this!"

3. Explain your choice. _____

_____

Review Listening Skills

How can words of encouragement show someone that you are listening?

Every conversation involves give and take. For true communication to take place, a conversation should also involve listening. Listening will help you share information with another person. It will help you work with your partner to solve problems.

When you listen, use positive body language. Sit forward, nod your head, and make eye contact. Use words of encouragement to show that you are listening.

Work to understand the speaker's ideas and feelings. Try repeating what the other person says, either exactly or in your own words. This practice gives both parties a chance to make things clear. It also shows that you are listening!

➤ Communication Builder

Read the following conversation between Nila and Lisa. Circle the examples of positive communication skills used by Nila.

Lisa and Nila sat down at a kitchen table. Nila took a deep breath to relax. She focused on her communication goal. She said to herself, "I will tell Lisa that I do not want to be part of her plan. I will stick to my decision."

"Lisa, I've been thinking about Saturday night," Nila began.

"Oh, I meant to thank you for helping me out," Lisa said. "You're a great friend!"

"Well, I'm glad you think so. But, I've decided I'm not comfortable with the plan. I don't want to tell your parents you're staying here if you are actually someplace else."

Lisa's jaw dropped. "You can't back out on me! Everything's settled!"

"I can see that you're upset, Lisa," Nila continued. "But, I just can't go along with it."

"You bet I'm upset, you little wimp! You're ruining all my plans!"

Nila felt herself starting to choke up. She took a deep breath. She kept her emotions under control.

"I know you're disappointed. But, I'm just not willing to go along with it. I don't believe in lying. I hope we can still be friends."

Lisa shook her head and stormed out the door. For a moment, Nila felt bad about letting her friend down. Then she was suddenly proud of herself. She had stuck to her goal! Lisa would not use her again. She hadn't let herself down! It was time to celebrate!

Chapter Summary

- Changing your communication style takes time, commitment, and practice. To change, you must be aware of your communication goals, body language, tone of voice, words, and how you listen. Then you must work to use these things in more positive ways.

- It's helpful to watch how others communicate. Look for positive communication skills that solve problems. Try to imitate these skills. Watch what happens when people communicate in an unhealthy way. Make an effort to avoid these mistakes.

- Identify your own communication goals. Then stick with these goals. Sometimes you will be successful and sometimes you won't. The main thing is to keep trying to communicate in a healthy way!

Chapter Review

Words to Know

Use your own words to describe the meaning of the word "conscious."

_____

About Communication

Answer each question in the space provided.

1. Why are communication goals important?

_____

_____

2. List two examples of positive body language.

_____

_____

3. What tone of voice matches the statement "I'm really happy for you"?

_____

_____

4. What is one way to show that you are listening?

_____

_____

5. Circle the statement that is the BEST way to tell a person how you feel.

   a. "You really make me mad!"

   b. "I'm really upset right now."

Communicating in a Healthy Way

Words to Know

Fill in each blank with a term listed below.

conversation	body language	communicate	express
attitude	conscious	emotion	encouragement
sincere	interpret	impression	instinct
negative	positive	message	react

1. When you _____, you explain the meaning of something.

2. A _____ person is truthful and honest.

3. A spoken exchange of ideas is a(n) _____.

4. An effect produced on your mind is a(n) _____.

5. _____ causes a baby to cry when hungry.

6. When you respond to what someone says or does, you _____ to that person.

7. _____ is how you use your body to communicate.

8. Your _____ is your manner of acting, thinking, or feeling.

9. When people share or exchange information, they _____.

10. Something that is harmful is _____.

11. The sender's _____ is the idea or the information that he or she wants to share with a listener.

12. Words of _____ give a person hope and support.

13. When you are _____ of an action, you know what you are doing.

14. Hate is a powerful _____.

15. When you are optimistic and hopeful, you are _____.

16. When you _____ yourself, you state your thoughts and feelings.

Ideas to Know

Answer each question in the space provided.

1. What three things are needed for communication to happen?

    _____

    _____

2. What effect does body language have on communication? Support your
    answer with examples.

    _____

    _____

    _____

3. What are three words or phrases a speaker might use to keep
    communication open and positive?

    _____

    _____

    _____

4. Identify three traits of a person who has a "listening attitude."

    _____

    _____

    _____

5. How has your communication style changed after reading this book?

    _____

    _____

    _____

Glossary

attitude: a person's way of acting, feeling, or thinking, 43

body language: how people use their bodies to communicate, 18

communicate: to share or exchange information or ideas, 6

conscious (KAHN-shuhs): knowing what one is doing and why, 56

conversation: a spoken exchange of information or ideas, 29

emotion (ih-MOH-shuhn): a strong feeling, such as love, hate, sadness, and anger, 32

encouragement (ihn-KEHR-ihj-muhnt): hope, confidence, or support, 45

express: to state one's thoughts or feelings, 30

impression (ihm-PREHSH-uhn): an effect produced on the mind or the feelings, 25

instinct: responses of people or animals which are not learned, but are inborn, 12

interpret (ihn-TEHR-priht): to explain or understand the meaning of something, 7

message: the idea or information that the sender wants to share with the listener, 6

negative: harmful; not helpful, 10

positive: constructive, optimistic, or hopeful, 10

react: to respond to what someone says or does, 31

sincere (sihn-SEER): truthful or honest, 45